Your Amazing Itty Bitty™ Divorce Handbook

15 Essential Tips to Help You Make the Best Decisions During the Worst of Times

Kathryn Costas, CDFA®

Published by Itty Bitty™ Publishing
A subsidiary of S & P Productions, Inc.

Your Amazing Itty Bitty™ Divorce Handbook
Second Edition

Printed in the United States of America

Itty Bitty Publishing
311 Main Street, Suite D
El Segundo, CA 90245
(310) 640-8885

ISBN: 978-1-959964-70-4

Finally! A Concise Comprehensive Divorce Guidebook

Learn From the Expert, and the 20/20 Hindsight of Hundreds of Divorces

The US divorce rate is close to 50%, and in California, it's close to 60%. In this easy-to-read, informative Itty Bitty™ book, Kathryn Costas provides an essential roadmap to help you successfully navigate the divorce process.

The 15 tips in this Itty Bitty™ book will guide you through every phase of the divorce process and provide you with the resources to make the best decisions during the worst of times.

You will learn:

- How to gather important financial information you will need
- How to assemble the perfect divorce team
- How to make smart decisions about the family home and key assets
- How to establish a parenting plan and set communication ground rules

Pick up a copy of this powerful book today and experience the confidence in knowing you have the tools you need to survive and thrive during and after your divorce.

Dedication Page

This book is dedicated to my children, Emily, Nick and Hailey, who are my reason for being. And to all the other angels in my life who carried me through my divorce and continue to love and guide me.

Stop by our Itty Bitty™ website to find interesting information regarding financial planning for divorce.

www.IttyBittyPublishing.com

Or visit **Kathryn Costas** at

https://www.epwealth.com/our-team/westlake-village/kathy-costas

or reach out to her directly at

kcostas@epwealth.com

Table of Contents

Introduction

This book is designed to serve as a guide so that you can avoid the mistakes of the many divorcing couples who have come before you. It is just the "20/20 hindsight" everyone wishes they had at the beginning of their divorce.

This book is for you if:

- You don't know how to determine the best first steps.
- You feel alone and overwhelmed by the financial decisions that need to be made and the steps that need to be taken to secure your financial future.
- You are worried about protecting your children's lifestyle and financial future.
- You are afraid your spouse has an unfair advantage in financial matters.
- Your current financial advisor is not a Certified Divorce Financial Analyst, CDFA®.

In most cases, divorce is a marathon, not a sprint. It involves twists and turns along the way and a few hills you may not have seen coming. Even on a smooth course, you need the right preparation for each step and a strong support team. Having the right information and expert professionals behind you will save you time and money and get you to a much better position at the finish line.

Whether it's deciding to keep or sell the house, or determining a fair division of assets, the tips in this book are designed to help. Your team should understand the emotions that surround these decisions, but with some guidance and expert advice, the right choices can be made.

Here are 15 essential tips that will help you include:

- Build a divorce team you can trust
- Gather the important financial information
- Set goals and determine the best settlement
- Create a sound financial strategy for your future

Sometimes taking that first step is the hardest. This book will take you by the hand and help you on your way. If you need additional information or resources, go to my website at:

https://www.epwealth.com/our-team/westlake-village/kathy-costas

Or reach out to me directly at kcostas@epwealth.com

Tip #1
Where Do I Start?

Hunt and Gather Your Financial Information. This first step will help you begin to see what you are entitled to and what your future financial picture might look like. If you do it well, it will save you time and money with an attorney or mediator. You should try to gather and organize all of your financial records from the past 3 years, including:

1. Personal and business tax returns
2. Most recent pay stubs for both of you
3. Banking and credit card statements
4. Mortgage statements
5. Investment account statements
6. Retirement account statements, including IRAs, 401(k)s and Pensions
7. Deferred compensation plans
8. All life insurance policies and annuities
9. Descriptions of employee benefits
10. A list of large property items
11. A full credit report that lists any and all debt
12. Any completed financial affidavits – listing of assets, liabilities, income and expenses for both of you

Things to Consider When Putting This Information Together

Knowledge is power. Now is the time to become informed; that is the inspiration behind this sometimes daunting task!

- If in doubt, include anything with a $ sign.
- Start watching the mail and paying attention to any financial statements that arrive, especially if you are not the one who usually deals with the money in your household.
- The more organized you are, the easier it will be for your attorney to use this information to protect your interests.
- If you have property or assets that were owned prior to marriage, do your best to find a paper trail that can document how and when the asset was acquired and why it is separate property.

Tip #2

Be A Team Player

It doesn't matter if you will be playing tackle football or just a chess match with your spouse; you owe it to yourself and your family to create a team to support you through this process. Your team should include a legal expert (attorney or mediator), a therapist and a certified divorce financial planning expert.

1. As with any life-changing decision, you should get at least two qualified opinions on the best way to settle your divorce.
2. Explore the option of mediation if you feel you can agree on the basics.
3. Spend the time and money up front on expert consultations. Don't just rely on the recommendation of friends or family.
4. Choose this next legal "partner" wisely. Trust and communication will be key. This person will be representing you and your family's best interests, and you may be working together for several months.
5. Find a therapist you feel most comfortable with.
6. Your financial expert should be a Certified Divorce Financial Analyst® who is trained and has experience with cases like yours.

Things to Consider When Building Your Team

- Each attorney or mediator has their own personality, style and strengths. Do your best to match the person and their firm with your case and your opponent's team.
- Mediation doesn't mean you agree on everything, just that you agree you don't want a judge deciding your future. This process is especially beneficial if you have young children together. You won't always be spouses, but you will always be parents.
- A Certified Divorce Financial Analyst® (CDFA®) is a valuable resource. They must pass a series of exams on all financial aspects of divorce and can testify as an expert witness in court if that is necessary.
- Treat your first meetings with all of these experts like a job interview. Ask them about their experience, ask for a timeline and estimate of costs, as well as a game plan and some "what ifs".
- Always rely on your friends and family for love and support, but not for legal or expert advice. Leave that to your qualified team members.

Tip #3
Money 101

All money is not created equal. Accurate valuations of all accounts are needed to determine what mix of assets is best for you. Start working with a CDFA® or other qualified divorce financial planner right away so you can learn about what you have and what you want.

1. Checking, savings and brokerage or investment accounts are usually the most liquid and easy to access and divide.
2. This is an important point if you will be needing extra cash to set up a new household, pay your attorney, etc.
3. Retirement accounts such as IRAs and 401(k)s are not considered liquid. There are often penalties and taxes on money taken out.
4. Retirement accounts, while not always liquid, are a very valuable savings tool for the future.
5. A CDFA® or financial planner should review all investment accounts, both taxable and retirement, to determine values, liquidity, tax implications and future growth potential.

Things to Consider About Money and Divorce

- While divorce is most often about the money, attorneys and mediators aren't qualified to give you financial planning advice. Attorneys go to law school; they are not financial planners. They will tell you what you are entitled to, but not necessarily what you really want based on your future.
- Solid financial advice is especially important if you are not the "money manager" in your marriage or if your spouse is the owner of a business that supports your family.
- While you may not be a numbers person or have experience with investments, you owe it to yourself and your children to start educating yourself and, most importantly, working with an advisor you trust. You will be making decisions during the divorce that will impact the rest of your life and possibly future generations.
- Divorce is a very emotional process. Treating it like a business decision is almost impossible. Rely on a trusted financial advisor to help you make logical decisions with your money, even when emotions are high.

Tip #4
The Divorce Diet

In any divorce, the "B" word, budget that is, should be used early and often. You wouldn't hire someone to remodel your kitchen without knowing what you could afford to spend and what part of the project was most important to you. Don't hire an attorney to remodel your life without having some idea what it might cost.

1. Keep in mind, a higher hourly rate does not necessarily equal a higher settlement or support number. It's more important to work with an attorney you trust and can communicate with.
2. A CDFA® can be instrumental in helping you determine what you can afford to spend and, more importantly, what is worth fighting for.
3. Ask about different ways to get the information you and your lawyer need. If you can do the legwork instead of your lawyer, you'll save hundreds of dollars or more.
4. Now is the time to get your personal spending under control as well. See more about this under Tip #7.

Things to Consider About Your Divorce Budget

- A lot of people lose weight without trying to during the divorce process. Unfortunately, without a budget to guide them, they also lose a lot of money they don't need to lose.
- Try to keep in mind that in a few years you will heal and start to move on. At that point, the big picture will be much more important than the coffee maker you spent $3,000 fighting for.
- Taking depositions and hiring forensic accountants are usually the most expensive "add-ons" to the divorce process. Make sure they are necessary to finding the answers you need.
- You may be told that you should treat this as a business deal. The problem is, it's not a business deal, it's your past, your present and your future.
- Hire an expert you trust to provide that logical analysis of your budget and do your best to listen to them.

Tip #5

Credit Where Credit Is Due

The one score you need to settle in your divorce is your Credit Score. Most of the focus in the divorce is on who gets what assets. Don't forget to figure out who owes what as well. While you're looking for hidden money, make sure you also look for hidden debt.

1. Pull your credit report from all three reporting agencies as soon as you decide to separate or divorce. A good free site is annualcreditreport.com.
2. It's important to account for all of these debts and determine if they are community debts or only belong to one of you.
3. Your overall FICO score is a good indication of your credit strength, but keep in mind that you have many FICO scores based on different formulas that are used for different purposes.
4. If you don't have any credit cards in just your name, now is the time to get one.
5. Don't close or cancel any joint credit cards that have a good credit history. That will erase all of the good history you have built. Just take one name off the card if at all possible.

Things to Consider About Your Credit Score

- The misuse of credit can be used as a weapon in divorce when one spouse refuses to pay a mortgage or other debt. This can impact both of you for several years. Make sure you have confirmation that bills are being paid if you aren't the one paying them.
- Your ability to get credit before you are divorced, but while you are separated, will be based on your household income, which includes the income from both of you. This is the number to use on any solo credit card applications, for example. That will change once you are officially divorced.
- If you are not the main wage earner, your credit score and history will be an even more important asset to you. From a rental application or mortgage application to getting a car loan, this score can make your future life easier or much more difficult.

Tip #6
The Kids Can Hear You

During the divorce, the parents need strict rules and firm limits. Divorce is a whole new territory in parenting. Consider meeting with a therapist at the beginning to lay the ground rules on communication with and around the kids. Words often become weapons in this battle, and they will leave a lasting mark. You both need to be clear on the best way to avoid wounding your children.

1. What may seem like a dig at your spouse can actually be interpreted by a child as blame on them.
2. Even if you can't agree on anything else, do your very best to be a united front on this aspect.
3. No matter what their age, kids do NOT want to be involved in this process in any way. This is your stuff, not theirs. Don't ask them to be a referee, a shoulder to cry on or a spy. They will resent having that burden put on them.
4. Remember, by definition, "family court" is charged with doing what's in the best interest of the children. Make sure your words and actions fall in that category, or you may suffer in court.

Things to Consider About Parenting During a Divorce

- Children come into the world with unconditional love for their parents. They are not wired to take sides. Don't try to make them. You would never want to be asked to choose one child over another. That is the same pain they will feel.
- Holding your tongue may take the greatest strength you've ever had to muster. But just like the small mother who lifts a car off of her child, you have the inner strength to do this. You will be saving their emotional life and your future relationship.
- Your kids should be off limits and never used as a bargaining chip. If that starts to happen, seek help immediately from a professional and get both of you back on the right track.

Tip #7

When One Becomes Two - Households That Is

If you're not a numbers person, you can always rely on your baking skills. Think of the money you have to run your household every month as a pie. Now you need to cut that pie into two pieces to represent the two households you will need to support going forward. This is the reality of divorce.

1. If custody will be 50/50, the goal of the court is to create two households with roughly equal funds available.
2. Based on simple math, division, not multiplication, is what is used to arrive at those numbers. Understanding this at the beginning of the process will help guide your expectations and could save you from wasting attorney fees down the road.
3. Now is the time to get a good handle on your monthly expenses and what it takes to run your household.
4. Compromises will likely need to be made on both sides in order to make this math work. Do your best to work together so you can keep your overall costs down.

Things to Keep in Mind About Creating Two Households

- If you are not used to managing money, this can feel overwhelming and scary. Rely on a CDFA® or other trusted advisor to help you track your expenses and manage costs. It will pay off during the process and get you started on the right foot once the divorce is done.
- Work with a therapist to determine how to discuss your new budget with your children. If it's appropriate, you can work with them to decide what expenses may have to be reduced. Sometimes, having a choice can be more important to them than what they may have to go without.
- Even if there is more than enough to go around at the outset, make sure you don't rely on retail therapy for you or to win favor with your children. Money spent from the community funds can be charged back against you, and you could end up owing money to your spouse.
- Most divorces cost more and take longer than you plan. Pace yourself and your spending so that you don't run out of steam or cash.

Tip #8
Xspouse - It's All About the Money

Beginning in 2025, the computer program in California that is used to calculate temporary spousal support (aka alimony or maintenance) and child support changed its name from Dissomaster to Xspouse. The goal and process remain essentially the same, however.

1. The goal of this program is to take the total after-tax income for both of you and divide it into 2 separate incomes that are roughly equal.
2. It is almost always used to determine the initial or temporary spousal support order and then may be fine-tuned in order to determine the permanent spousal support order.
3. Child support in most states is determined by this type of calculator. Child support is not taxable to the recipient and is not a tax deduction to the payor. It can be modified up or down based on a material financial change for either party.
4. Spousal support is also non-taxable at the federal level, but the amount can be negotiated or even given as a lump sum.

Things to Keep in Mind About Xspouse

- This particular tool is only used in California. Other states use different methods to calculate both child and spousal support.
- Because this is just a computer program, the numbers it generates are only as good as the data used for input. Make sure you and your attorney understand and agree with each line item before you agree to a support order that the program generates.
- Keep in mind that it takes a relatively large shift in custodial time and/or income in order to have a significant impact on the support order. Have your attorney run several different scenarios, so you know your best and worst case.
- In California, the final orders for spousal support from a judge are generally 15-20% lower than what the Xspouse spits out. Make sure you keep that fact in mind when you're negotiating or deciding whether or not to go to trial.
- Unlike spousal support that is set based on the marital standard of living, child support can be adjusted upward if either spouse has a windfall or a significant, positive change in income. You are no longer spouses, but you are always parents, and the children should benefit from a better financial scenario.

Tip #9

A Better Way Than Right Down The Middle

Typically, the method to divide assets in a community property state and often an equitable distribution state, is to split each community asset right down the middle. There are often much better ways to do this from a financial planning point of view.

1. Create an inventory of all assets, both community and separate. The separate assets you have could make certain community assets more or less valuable.
2. Work with your CDFA® or tax professional to make sure you know the tax implications of all assets before you enter into any negotiations (see Tip #3 for more on this).
3. Your tax bracket and financial needs will change during different phases of your life. Your CDFA® can create cash flow projections to make sure the assets you are negotiating for have the tax treatment and liquidity to best meet these needs.
4. Do your best not to be emotionally tied to one asset. This can happen with the family home. Evaluate what you are giving up for each asset you choose.

Things to Keep in Mind When Deciding How to Divide Assets

- Your assets may have different long-term values for each of you, depending on your current and future earning capacity, as well as separate property. This often provides an opportunity to get creative in the division and make both of you better off in light of your post-divorce goals and needs.
- Like all of these crucial steps and decisions, knowledge is power. First, determine your goals and needs during the different periods of your life, then make sure you understand what assets will best support them.
- There are a lot of variables to pull together, but your CDFA® or other qualified financial professional can use sophisticated financial projection software to explore different scenarios and determine what is best for you. This is the time to use your team.

Tip #10
What About Your Home?

Your home is filled with memories and emotions. For this reason, it is often a major point of contention during a divorce. Use your CDFA® to help you make the best decision about this asset. You don't want to fight for a home you can't afford to keep. You will lose twice.

1. Maintenance on a larger home can end up being an albatross. Do the cash flow analysis that includes the mortgage, property taxes, HOA fees, insurance, maintenance, etc., so you know whether you can afford to stay. You will also need a cash reserve set aside for unforeseen expenses or major repairs.
2. Determine the cost of alternative housing. It may be cheaper to stay in the house if you have a small mortgage.
3. One spouse can't just assume the mortgage from the other spouse. It is considered a refinance at current rates and with the full approval process.
4. Capital gains tax on the sale of the home is another major point to consider. If you have a lot of equity, you will keep more of it if you sell the house when you are still both owners.

Things to Keep in Mind About Your Home

- Many parents feel it is important to keep the house if there are children still living there. They are hoping to maintain some stability for the kids during a large life change. Just make sure this decision doesn't result in a huge financial strain and potential loss of the home a few years later.
- To help you determine your options, work with a trusted mortgage professional to see what you would qualify for. Many mortgage lenders will consider spousal and child support as income as long as the order has been in effect for 3-6 months and will continue for the next 3 years. There are also lenders who will calculate an asset depletion schedule if you receive a lump sum buyout or other large sum of cash or investments.
- Generally speaking, children feel stability and comfort when both parents are calm, happy and not stressed about money. Use this as your guide when deciding on the home.
- If you decide that selling the home is best for everyone, involve the children in selecting the next home. You might be surprised how excited they will get when they have an opportunity to pick their new room or neighborhood.

Tip #11
Gray Divorce - With Age Comes Complexity

In the last 10 years, the divorce rate among people over 50 has skyrocketed. There are several reasons for this, including more financially independent women, longer lifespans and Viagra, to name a few. Divorce during retirement or even as it approaches brings additional complexity and the need to be creative in negotiating a viable settlement.

1. Retirement almost always means a smaller, fixed income for both parties to live on. This may mean a very small spousal support order or perhaps none at all.
2. The marital home may be the most valuable asset you both own. Finding a solution for how to divide this asset can be even more difficult. You may need to consider a reverse mortgage or over-55 neighborhoods for options to keep a roof over both of your heads.
3. Health care costs tend to rise at this age, and often, couples who aren't quite Medicare age decide to opt for Legal Separation over divorce to allow one spouse to remain a dependent for medical benefit coverage qualification.

Things to Keep in Mind About Gray Divorce

- Creating a stable cash flow for both parties will be paramount. Make sure pensions are valued properly and all payout options are considered. And don't forget income from RMDs for long-term planning.
- Reach out to the Social Security Administration to determine your benefit and the spousal benefit you are entitled to. Claiming on an ex-spouse's benefit does not affect that spouse's benefit at all. You can receive the greater of your benefit or half of your spouse's starting at age 62 as long as you were married for 10 years, have been divorced for 2 years and your spouse has reached their full retirement age.
- Retirement accounts are often one of the largest assets to divide. The initial division isn't taxable, but keep in mind that all money taken out is taxed as ordinary income, so that needs to be factored into your cash flow.
- Keep existing life insurance policies in force, and if possible, each spouse as a beneficiary. These are very valuable assets that often can't be replaced.

Tip #12
Forensic Accountants And Other Specialists – Do You Need Them?

Much like a medical condition, the more complex the issues in the divorce, the more likely you will need additional specialists. The difficult part is being able to make an informed decision about the need to involve them and incur added costs.

1. The most common specialist is a forensic accountant. They are vital to establishing the value of a business as well as tracing funds if there is money moving from account to account. They are also used to verify separate property claims, determine the marital standard of living and income available for support.
2. Another common specialist is the QDRO attorney. They specialize in creating the legal documents that divide Qualified Plans such as 401(k)s, pension plans or deferred compensation plans.
3. If you are in a custody battle, you may need to hire a custody evaluator. They are usually therapists who determine the best custody arrangement.
4. Vocational evaluators can be necessary to determine the income potential of a spouse.

Things to Keep in Mind About Hiring Specialists

- The common misconception about forensic accountants is that they act as detectives to find hidden money. The reality is, they use the information provided by each of you to create a financial snapshot.
- Private investigators are the ones who act as detectives to gather information. They conduct asset searches to see if there is money that your spouse is hiding. They can also make sure you aren't being spied on by your spouse through your phone, computer, car, or even cameras and microphones in your home.
- Another common misconception about forensic specialists is that they give you financial advice. They give you a balance sheet that lists all of your assets and debts as of a certain date, but they don't tell you which assets you want, what those assets will be worth in 5 or 10 years or how much money you will have to live on after taxes. That is the job of your CDFA®, another important specialist to include on your team.
- Don't be afraid to speak up and ask your attorney why you need a specialist. Make sure it isn't just part of their process. However, if necessary, you will likely be very glad you brought them in.

Tip #13
No Such Thing As Forever With Spousal Support

Just like in a marriage, there are no guarantees that spousal support will last forever. Even if there is no official end date to the order, circumstances can arise that reduce or end those payments.

1. A spousal support order is determined by the ability to pay, need for support, limits on the ability of the recipient to earn income, marital lifestyle, findings of domestic violence and several other factors. The death of either spouse causes an end to support, as does remarriage, and in some cases, cohabitation.
2. In many states, spousal support for a marriage of less than 10 years lasts for half the length of the marriage. For marriages longer than 10 years, there is often no official end date, but certain changes can end it immediately or reduce it over time.
3. Increasingly, the courts are expecting both parties to be working toward financial independence without support.
4. There are also unforeseen events, such as job loss or disability of the payor, that end or reduce support.

Things to Keep in Mind About Spousal Support Orders

- Most support orders are modifiable and can be changed when one party retires or changes jobs, etc.
- Don't try to spend more to increase the marital lifestyle number in an attempt to get more support. You will just end up depleting assets, and you'll have less money in the end. You may also owe money back to the other spouse. Support is based primarily on the income coming in, not what is spent. Keep that in mind.
- No matter what the circumstance, it is important for you to make efforts to become financially self-sufficient or at least to provide a supplemental income source as a backup to a support order. Things happen in life, and both spouses should do their best to protect their financial well-being.
- Becoming financially independent should be seen as a reward, not a punishment. It will allow you to have complete freedom from your spouse and provide for a future that you design all on your own.

Tip #14
Ways To Secure Your Final Judgment

The final divorce judgment is just a piece of paper. You need to take steps to make it more powerful than that and to cover the "what ifs".

1. Life insurance should be part of any settlement that includes a child support order. The goal is to have a death benefit that is large enough to replace the support in case the payor passes away.
2. Disability insurance is another important form of protection. Someone in their 40s is far more likely to become disabled than to die. This is especially important for certain professionals who rely on their physical capabilities to earn income.
3. If the settlement includes another ongoing payment obligation, such as a note payable over time, be sure this obligation is made into a legal Note, and both of you sign it. The Note should be secured by some other asset as well.
4. Don't be afraid to use a wage garnishment order to collect on a support order. It isn't difficult to set up and can actually be easier for both of you, in that there is no need to write a check twice a month.

Things to Keep in Mind About Securing Your Support Order

- With life insurance, ideally, the policy should be standalone, not through an employer, so that it does not disappear if the job does. Also, the recipient of support should be added as a second notice so that if a premium isn't paid, you will know before the policy terminates.
- Another great child support enforcement tool in California and other states is the Department of Child Support Services. The DCSS will enforce a garnishment order and monitor all payments. They can seize other assets if support is not paid, and best of all, this service is completely FREE.
- You've worked so hard to get to a final agreement. Don't lose the value of all of that work by not completing these final steps.
- A CDFA® is a great resource to help you with these final steps. The attorney's job is finished with the judgment. A CDFA® will help you move accounts and monitor payments, and make sure all of the financial details are covered and secured. Take a breath and push through this last step with a CDFA® helping out. You'll be very glad you did.

Tip #15
If You Have Children, It's Never Final

You won't always be spouses, but you will always be parents. Make plans now and set expectations for the future that will help your whole family as you transition from one household to two.

1. The custody arrangement written into your settlement is based on the current ages of your children. As they get older and have different priorities and more rigorous school demands, try to agree to be somewhat flexible with your plans.
2. Work with a parenting coach to help you anticipate changes with your children and facilitate the flexibility that might be required. Communication will be key, and since you will be living apart, that can be more difficult.
3. Make a plan to cover expenses for the kids' activities. Consider funding an account each school year with an agreed amount and contribution percentage to cover these costs.
4. One of the biggest financial goals parents have is a college education. Make plans now and set financial targets so you are both clear about the expectations you both have.

Things to Keep in Mind About Parenting After a Divorce

- There are apps such as www.2houses.com and www.ourfamilywizard.com that provide shared calendars and an email tool to help you work together. This can be another great way to keep the lines of communication open for parenting.
- Don't forget the final act of parenting, which is creating an estate plan. You will need a trust to make sure your children are the recipients of your assets, as well as a guardianship plan in case this transfer happens when they are young. It's not something you want to think about, but once done, the peace of mind it gives you that you are taking care of your children forever makes it worth it.
- As time goes on and emotions fade, there will be graduations, weddings and births that you will both want to be a part of. Agree to work together as parents so you and your children can enjoy these milestones.

You've finished. Before you go…

Post/share that you finished this book.

Please star rate this book.

Reviews are solid gold to writers. Please take a few minutes to give us some itty bitty feedback.

ABOUT THE AUTHOR

Kathryn Costas

Going through my own six-year divorce inspired me to turn that bad experience into something good. I saw a big need for financial planning advice during and after divorce, and knew that was the way I could use my “lemons” to help others make “lemonade”. I have found my passion and my purpose!

I began my career in financial services in 2008 and am now an Investment Advisor as well as a CDFA® or Certified Divorce Financial Analyst®. This credential allows me to provide solid financial planning advice in the context of divorce. I use this education and my personal experience to serve as a compassionate guide to help clients successfully navigate the financial aspects of the divorce process.

I am always working to learn more and be a great resource to my clients. I am the LA area Chapter Chair of the Divorce Alliance, a member of the Conejo Divorce Resource Group, and a presenter for the Second Saturday and Divorce Cares groups in Ventura County. I am also very active with the Cystic Fibrosis Foundation and as a member of the local chapter of Together Women Rise and a Board Member for Childhood Matters.

My work can be exhausting and emotionally draining, but there is no greater reward in life than watching someone emerge from fear and sadness into confidence and happiness!

Going through my own divorce and helping hundreds of other people navigate the process as a CDFA® has given me a unique perspective and skill set to help others have an even better result.

My goal for this book is to give the reader some guidance so that they can make the best decisions possible for themselves and their family.

I hope to provide enough answers and also prompt enough questions to keep the reader from making the same mistakes others have made, so that they can emerge from the process with confidence and optimism about the future.

If you enjoyed this Itty Bitty™ book, you might also like…

- **Your Amazing Itty Bitty™ Financial Fitness Book** – Akemi Clauson
- **Your Amazing Itty Bitty™ Affirmations Book** – Micaela Passeri
- **Becoming A Victor** – B.A. Victor

Or any of the many Amazing Itty Bitty™ books available online at www.ittybittypublishing.com

www.ingramcontent.com/pod-product-compliance
Lightning Source LLC
LaVergne TN
LVHW022324200926
848481LV00004B/1423
9781959964704